UNCOVERING HISTORY
THE RENAISSANCE

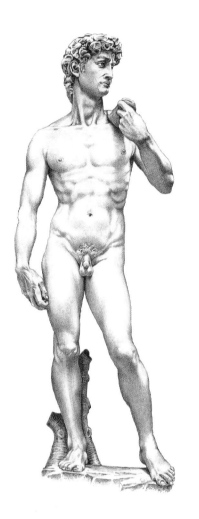

Everyday Life in the Renaissance
was created and produced by McRae Books Srl
Borgo Santa Croce, 8 – 50122 – Florence (Italy)
info@mcraebooks.com
www.mcraebooks.com

ISBN 88-89272-58-9

SERIES EDITOR Anne McRae
TEXT Antony Mason
CONSULTANT Sabine Eiche
MAIN ILLUSTRATIONS MM comunicazione (Manuela Cappon, Monica Favilli) ps. 19, 22, 24–25, 28–29, 32–33, 40–41; Luisa della Porta p.12; Giacinto Gaudenzi ps. 42–43, 44–45; Lucia Mattioli ps. 20–21; Paola Ravaglia ps. 14–15, 27, 34, 36–37; Andrea Ricciardi di Gaudesi ps. 16–17; Claudia Saraceni ps. 11, 30–31, 38; Sergio ps. 8–9
ILLUSTRATIONS Lorenzo Cecchi, Giampiero Mangialardi, Lucia Mattioli, Studio Stalio (Alessandro Cantucci, Fabiano Fabbrucci, Margherita Salvadori)
MAPS Paola Baldanzi
GRAPHIC DESIGN Marco Nardi
DESIGNER Rebecca Milner
PROJECT EDITOR Claire Moore
REPRO Litocolor, Florence

Printed and bound in Italy

UNCOVERING HISTORY

Antony Mason

EVERYDAY LIFE IN THE
RENAISSANCE

Illustrations by MM comunicazione, Luisa della Porta, Giacinto Gaudenzi, Lucia Mattioli, Paola Ravaglia, Andrea Ricciardi di Gaudesi, Claudia Saraceni, Sergio, Studio Stalio

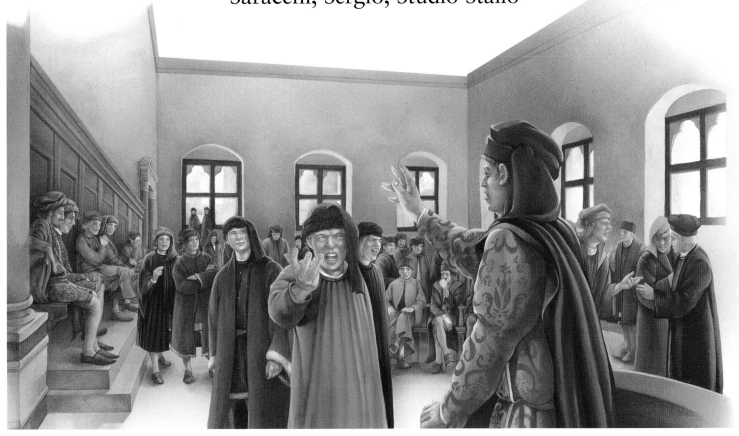

McRae Books

Table of Contents

Introduction

The Renaissance was a period of great change in Europe. Between the early 1300s and the late 1500s Europe was transformed from a medieval world to something beginning to resemble the modern world. The term 'Renaissance' (French for 're-birth') was used by later historians because, looking back, it seemed that Europe had been reborn and re-energized after nearly 1,000 years of stagnation since the collapse of the Roman Empire.

During the Renaissance, scholars, architects and artists rediscovered just how advanced the ancient Greeks and Romans had been. Intrigued and enthused by this, they studied ancient Greek and Roman writing, science, sculpture and ruins, and used this knowledge to seek improvements in all aspects of their own lives. The original source of these changes was Italy, where the enlightened rulers of small but rich city-states, notably Florence, encouraged their scholars and artists to recreate the achievements of the Greeks and Romans. People of exceptional brilliance, such as Leonardo da Vinci, became totally absorbed by painting, sculpture, architecture, music and scientific research — displaying multi-talented interests that gave birth to the concept of the 'Renaissance Man'.

The achievements of Renaissance ideas, art and architecture spread quickly across Europe through international trade and travel, the universities and the new technology of printing. This Renaissance spirit of enquiry and questioning also gave rise to the Protestant clash with the Roman Catholic Church, and by the end of the 16th century, religious strife dominated all aspects of politics, learning and culture. The Renaissance was over, but it had changed the world.

Chronology of the Renaissance

LIFE OF PETRARCH, THE ITALIAN POET WHO MARKS THE START OF THE RENAISSANCE
1304–74

THE BLACK DEATH DEVASTATES EUROPE
1347–52

BRUNELLESCHI'S DOME OF FLORENCE CATHEDRAL IS BUILT
1420–1436

LIFE OF LORENZO DE' MEDICI, WHICH COINCIDES WITH A HIGHPOINT OF THE RENAISSANCE IN FLORENCE
1449–92

GUTENBERG PUBLISHES HIS BIBLE, THE FIRST PRINTED BOOK IN EUROPE
1455

LIFE OF ERASMUS, WHICH COINCIDES WITH THE FLOWERING OF NORTHERN EUROPEAN HUMANISM
1469–1536

CHRISTOPHER COLUMBUS REACHES THE AMERICAS
1492

LEONARDO DA VINCI, MICHELANGELO AND RAPHAEL BRING THE TRENDS IN ART TO A PEAK IN THE HIGH RENAISSANCE
c.1490–c.1530

MARTIN LUTHER PUBLISHES HIS NINETY-FIVE THESES, MARKING THE START OF THE PROTESTANT REVOLUTION
1517

REIGN OF FRANCIS I BRINGS THE RENAISSANCE TO FRANCE
1515–47

HAND-HELD FIREARMS ARE USED IN THE BATTLE OF PAVIA
1525

ANDREAS VESALIUS PUBLISHES HIS LANDMARK BOOK ON ANATOMY
1543

THE COUNCIL OF TRENT LAUNCHES THE COUNTER-REFORMATION
1545–63

THE GLOBE THEATRE IS BUILT IN LONDON
1598–9

Renaissance Origins

No one can say for sure when the Renaissance began, but it was in the cities of northern Italy that the first signs were seen. By the mid-1400s, the Renaissance was in full swing in Italy, reaching a peak during the 'High Renaissance' between c.1490 and c.1530. However, some people say that it began well before this, in the days of the Italian poet Petrarch (1304–74), who pioneered a revival of interest in the literature of Classical Antiquity — ancient Greece and Rome.

In the 1400s Italy was divided into small states around the main cities.

Classical humanism

During the early Renaissance, scholars studied the Classical literature of Greek and Roman times and were surprised by what they found. The ancient literature showed a profound understanding of the world and humanity. Inspired by this, 'humanist' scholars began to question the teachings of the Church and to look at the world in a new light.

Petrarch (left) is sometimes called the 'father of humanism'. He owned the largest collection of Classical writings of his time.

Disease and war

The medieval world was often unpredictable, violent and bleak. The bubonic plague (Black Death), which swept across Europe between 1347 and 1352, killed between one-fourth and one-third of the entire population. Meanwhile, the Hundred Years' War consumed the energies of England and France from 1337 to 1453. The Renaissance was in part a reaction to these events, and in part the search for better ways to govern states and to improve society.

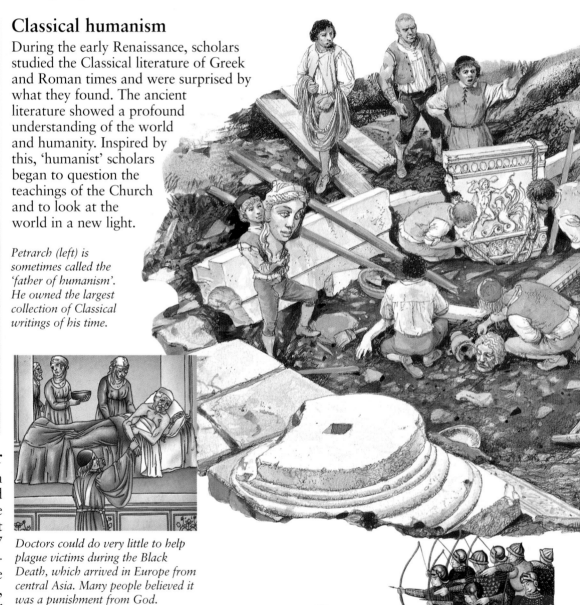

Doctors could do very little to help plague victims during the Black Death, which arrived in Europe from central Asia. Many people believed it was a punishment from God.

Some 6,000 French soldiers died at the Battle of Agincourt in 1415, a famous victory for the English king, Henry V, in his attempt to claim the French throne during the Hundred Years' War.

Architects and artists drew and measured the Classical antiquities in Rome, adapting the designs for their own buildings and sculptures.

The Italian painter Andrea Mantegna (c.1431–1506) often visited the ancient ruins in Rome. He tried to recreate a Roman city scene in this detail from his painting San Sebastiano *(right).*

Birthplace of the Renaissance

The Renaissance began in Italy. Being the homeland of the Roman Empire, there was still plenty of evidence of its achievements — in ruins, sculpture and writing. By the 1400s, Italian city-states, such as Florence and Venice, had become wealthy through trade, crafts and banking, while among the upper classes, it was fashionable to spend money on buildings, art, poetry, music and scholarship.

Many of the greatest works of sculpture in ancient Rome were by Greek sculptors, such as the famous statue of Laocoön (below), dating from the 1st century AD. *It was dug up in Rome in 1506.*

Collectors

Wealthy people of Renaissance Italy made collections of ancient sculpture and other artifacts, such as coins, pottery and glassware. They put them on show in their 'cabinet galleries', or *studioli*, alongside new works on Classical themes, commissioned from living artists. A brisk trade in antiques soon developed, encouraging people to dig and look for more.

Artistic stimulation

Rome had the richest collection of ruins and remains from Classical Antiquity. During the 1400s artists and architects travelled to the city to study what had survived. Filippo Brunelleschi (1377–1446), the architect of the famous dome of Florence Cathedral (see pages 16–17), spent several years in Rome, sometimes accompanied by Donatello (c.1386–1466), the first major Renaissance sculptor.

Renaissance collectors displayed their antique treasures to encourage discussion, as well as admiration for their artistic taste.

Italian Rule

During the medieval period, most of Europe was ruled by the feudal system. Feudal lords ran large agricultural estates, benefiting from the work of peasants while providing them with protection. However, after vast numbers of workers were lost during the Black Death, power switched from the feudal estates to the towns and cities. By Renaissance times, Italian city-states such as Florence and Siena had strong, democratic governments.

A portrait of Federico da Montefeltro, Duke of Urbino, painted in 1476–77, depicts him as both a warrior and a scholar.

Siena's Town Hall, with its soaring bell tower, has always been a symbol of the city's pride.

The ruling families

In Renaissance times, wealthy families dominated the Italian cities. Some were merchant and banking families, such as the Medici of Florence. Others were nobles and dukes, such as the Este family of Ferrara, the Gonzaga of Mantua, the Sforza of Milan and the Montefeltro of Urbino, some of whom had gained power by military force. In Rome, the popes were chosen from among these leading families. All were interlinked by an intricate game of politics, rivalries, conspiracy and marriage.

Below: A detail of a mural in the Medici Palace Chapel in Florence, called the Journey of the Magi, which is said to include portraits of the Medici family.

Machiavelli was a diplomat for the government of Florence.

Civic pride

For much of the Renaissance there was fierce competition among cities to build the most beautiful town halls, palaces and churches. This civic pride was particularly strong in Italy, where the city-states were frequently at war with each other.

Social structure

Much of the wealth of the Italian cities was generated by a growing middle-class of merchants, professionals, craftsmen and artisans. They had a powerful influence on the way their cities were run. They also helped those less fortunate than themselves by funding charities, hospitals, schools and poorhouses.

Below: A ceramic plaque by the Florentine sculptor Giovanni della Robbia shows a rich man giving food to the poor.

Before an election, the names of candidates for high offices in Florence were placed in ballot bags like these.

Italian republics and city-states

Medieval feudal rule was less rigid in the cities, where merchants and artisans enjoyed the freedom granted by feudal lords under charters. By the 14th century, many cities in Italy had developed their own systems of self-government. Some were republics, run by city councils, and others were ruled by despots. In his influential book *The Prince*, the Italian writer Niccolò Machiavelli (1469–1527) suggested that ruthless tactics may be the best way to achieve and retain power.

Hanging was a common form of execution in Renaissance
times, used for crimes such as murder and repeated theft.

Good government

Renaissance humanists frequently discussed what made a good or bad
government, and studied how Classical authors, such as Plato, had
addressed the question. Venice's stable and strong government was
much admired. It was controlled by the Grand Council, who elected the
doge and the Senate. In Florence, the centre of government was at the
Palazzo Vecchio, built in 1299 as the home of the guilds.
Members of the Florentine guilds gathered
here to discuss city issues and to vote,
but democracy diminished as the
Medici family's power grew.

Law and order

The Renaissance cities of Italy inherited
the traditions of Roman law, which was
dispensed by judges through courts.
However, justice was inconsistent and often
corrupt, and torture was widely used to gain
a confession. The main punishments were
fines or — for many offences — the death
penalty. Prison served mainly as a
temporary measure, not as a punishment
in itself. Separate Church courts held
trials for heresy and witchcraft.

A detail of Sano di Pietro's Allegory of Good
Government shows Liberty, holding a globe,
assisted by two diligent civil servants.

The doge of Venice was elected for life,
but his powers were limited. He was
usually chosen from one of the leading
Venetian families.

Below: A political
meeting takes place in
the Sala dei Dugento
(Hall of the Two
Hundred) in the
Palazzo Vecchio.

Banking and Trade

The Renaissance was also a time of major economic change in Europe. In place of agriculture, manufacturing and trade were becoming the new sources of wealth. Merchants exploited every opportunity to make a profit. The first stock exchange began in Bruges in the 1200s, and the idea soon spread to other European cities. By the 1300s, banking had become a complex and highly profitable business. Meanwhile, the guilds formed powerful political forces in the cities.

This 14th century document from the Florence coiners' guild shows florins aligned with the halo of the city's patron saint, John the Baptist.

The arms of Peruzzi (top) and Bardi (right) bankers. The Peruzzi and Bardi banks went bankrupt in the 1340s after King Edward III of England failed to pay back loans for his war in France.

Above: Italian moneylenders carry out their business.

Banking

In medieval times, bankers were simply moneylenders, but by the Renaissance period banking was much more complex. Bankers changed currencies, collected debts and provided cash for wages. The big banks were international firms, with branches in many of the major European cities. Their clients included not only wealthy traders and businessmen, but also kings, princes, bishops and popes.

A German banker at work. By the early 1500s, they had become the dominant bankers of Europe. Renaissance bankers dealt not only in coins, but also in gems and bills of exchange — written promises to pay money, which predated the invention of paper money.

Merchants and trade

During the Renaissance, trade routes criss-crossed Europe and the Mediterranean Sea and had links with the Far East. Venice was the most powerful trading city in the world. Its merchants controlled trade with the eastern Mediterranean, where they bought valuable goods such as silk from China, carpets from Persia and spices from Indonesia. These luxury goods ended up in wealthy homes in London and Bruges, along with furs from Russia and wine from France.

The network of trade routes across Europe carried luxury goods, wool, wine, coal and dried fish.

——— Hanseatic trade route
——— Genoese trade route
——— Venetian trade route

Wool workers prepare the raw material of the cloth industry.

Below: A ceramic medallion by Luca della Robbia shows the lamb, symbol of the wool guild.

Guilds

Almost every trade had a guild — a kind of trade union to protect the interests of tradesmen and their families, control wages and prices, set standards for training and for the quality of their goods. Each guild had a guildhouse, its headquarters, as well as a chapel dedicated to its patron saint.

In an age when most people could not read, guilds were often represented by pictures of the tools of the trade, such as scissors and razors for barbers, and an axe for carpenters.

Industry and crafts

Brewing beer, boat-building, baking, making weapons, armour, candles, barrels, baskets or furniture — these, and many more, were important trades in the Renaissance period. The cloth trade, however, was the most important of all. Raw wool was made into fine textiles and tapestries. One of the biggest buildings at the centre of many Renaissance cities was the cloth hall, where cloth was traded.

Many trades were family businesses, as seen in this print of a Dutch shoemaker's workshop (left).

Currency

The most secure form of money were coins of gold and silver. The gold *fiorino*, or florin, from Florence was one of the most trusted coins, and was used internationally. Venice had equally reliable gold ducats, stamped with an image of the doge. Other Renaissance coins contained a mixture of metals; their value could be trusted only if produced and stamped by a respected mint.

A Venetian ducat featuring the doge kneeling before St. Mark, the patron saint of Venice.

Wealthy banking families

In Renaissance times, Italian bankers — and in particular the bankers of Florence, such as the Bardi, Peruzzi and Medici — were the richest and most powerful in Europe. Banks were run by families, with the business passing down from father to son. The Italian banks — apart from those in Genoa — lost their dominance in the late 1400s, and their place was taken by German banking families, notably the Fugger and the Welser.

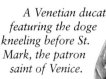

In 1473 Jakob Fugger (left) became chief banker to the Habsburgs, the ruling family of Austria and much of Europe.

The Printing Revolution

In 1450, Johannes Gutenberg revealed a technological breakthrough to the world. In his workshop in Mainz he began to print books using moveable type. By 1455 he had printed over 200 copies of the Latin Bible. Before this, all books had to be hand-copied. With printing, however, it was possible to make many copies of whole books in just a few days. It meant that new books, new translations and new ideas, often illustrated with pictures and maps, spread quickly through Europe. Printing was perhaps the single most important development of the Renaissance.

A medieval carving shows a monk copying a book with a reed pen. Copying books by hand made them both costly and rare.

Early book production

Before Gutenberg's invention, it would have taken many months for scribes to copy a single book by hand. This system rapidly declined after the development of printing with moveable type. However, Gutenberg did not invent printing as such. Prints had been made from woodblocks for hundreds of years. Almost 600 years before Gutenberg, the Chinese had printed books by carving woodblocks into pages of text and pictures.

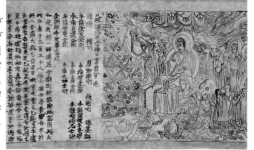

Right: A detail of the frontispiece of the Diamond Sutra, *the earliest known book, printed in China from woodblocks in AD 868.*

Gutenberg's invention

Gutenberg's real breakthrough was to find a method of mass-producing letters in a durable alloy of metal. By making sets of individual letters, printers could create a whole page of type, instead of carving a page as one piece. The typeset pages could later be broken up and the letters used again. His very first printed book was the Bible, a huge undertaking, which impressed people for its clarity.

Right: Gutenberg (c.1398–1468) and a copy of his Bible. His team worked for many years in secret, fearing that someone else would steal his idea.

Printing around Europe

Gutenberg's invention caught on rapidly. Within a few years, printing workshops were set up in Italy, France, England, the Netherlands and Poland. William Caxton (c.1422–91) first saw printing in Cologne. He published the first printed book in English in Bruges in 1475, before setting up the first printing press in England a year later. By 1500, some 40,000 books had been published in Europe.

Right: Caxton's colophon, dating from about 1487. Each printer had his own 'colophon' or emblem.

Many more women learned to read with the invention of printing. Margaret Roper (left), daughter of the English humanist Sir Thomas More, translated many works into English.

The spread of knowledge

Initially, printers produced books for scholars, the Church and wealthy patrons — books on grammar, philosophy, science, religion and law. From the start they also saw a market for general readers and produced tales of adventure and romance, history, fables, travel books, almanacs, encyclopaedias and sheet music. Translations of works by the ancient Latin and Greek authors were also very popular. By the early 1500s virtually all known Classical works had been published in printed editions.

Left: Some early printers tried to imitate the style of medieval manuscripts, as seen from this page printed in 1477.

Printers' workshops were often fairly small, with just one or two presses. Each press could produce about 16 printed pages an hour. Some printers bound their books in covers, others handed this task over to specialist bookbinders. Many printers also acted as booksellers.

Left: The printer checks a printed sheet for the quality and clarity of the impression.

Right: Workers in a paper mill in the 1500s.

Above: At the printing press, a printer's assistant pulls on the handle of the screw-spindle, lowering the platen, which presses the paper firmly onto the page of type.

Preparing the type

The first task of a printer using Gutenberg's system was to create the type. A letter was carved in reverse on the end of a steel rod to make a 'punch', which was then hammered into softer metal to make a mould. A molten metal alloy was then poured into the mould to make copies of the original letter. Trays of letters, plus punctuation marks, would be placed beside the typesetter, whose job it was to copy a text word for word. The pages of completed text would then be secured in a frame and placed on the flat bed of the press for printing.

Above: A printer inks the pages of type on the bed of the press. Behind him, typesetters select letters to make up the pages of type.

Paper

As the printing industry developed, there was a rise in demand for paper. Many hand-copied books had been written on parchment (animal skin), which was unsuitable for printing. Paper, often made from the pulp of rags, wood and other natural fibres, was cheaper. The technique of papermaking, invented in China over 1,000 years earlier, had reached Europe in about 1150.

Italian Renaissance Architecture

Architecture was perhaps the most visible of all the changes that took place during the Renaissance. This was particularly true in Italy, where Renaissance buildings dominated the skyline of many of its cities, such as Florence Cathedral and St. Peter's Basilica in Rome. Outside Italy, architects borrowed Renaissance ideas about Classical architecture to decorate their buildings, but few complete Renaissance-style buildings were constructed until the 1600s.

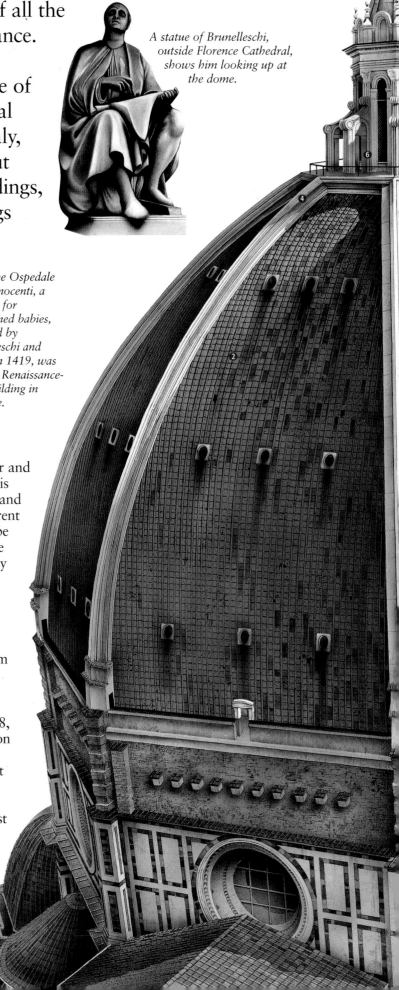

A statue of Brunelleschi, outside Florence Cathedral, shows him looking up at the dome.

Left: The Ospedale degli Innocenti, a hospital for abandoned babies, designed by Brunelleschi and begun in 1419, was the first Renaissance-style building in Florence.

Renaissance style

The architects of the Renaissance were attracted to the grandeur and elegance of Classical buildings. Many features contributed to this effect, including mathematically precise proportions, symmetry and strong horizontal lines. Other important features included different orders (styles of columns) and the pediment (the triangular shape placed under the roof, usually over an entrance). These were the features of Greek and Roman temples, but they were adapted by Renaissance architects for both civic and religious buildings.

Florence Cathedral

Florence Cathedral, started in 1296, took many decades to build. A problem arose over how to contruct the dome above the huge octagon at the eastern end of the cathedral. No dome of this size had ever been built before. In 1418, Filippo Brunelleschi proposed a solution based on his studies of Gothic and Roman architecture and his own talent for engineering. Built in 16 years, without using internal scaffolding for support, the dome is one of the greatest masterpieces of Renaissance architecture.

Brunelleschi designed a number of ingenious mechanical aids, such as this huge crane (left), to help in the construction of the dome.

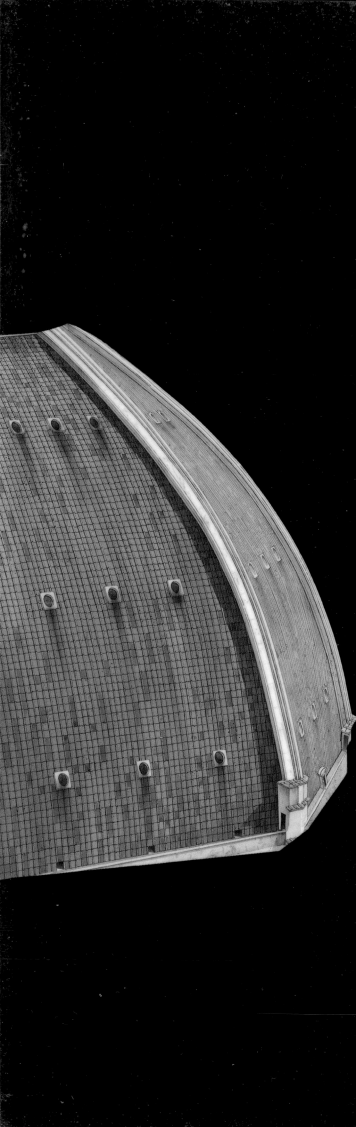

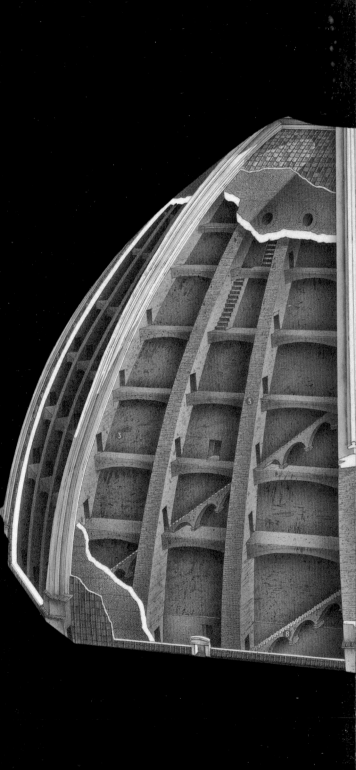

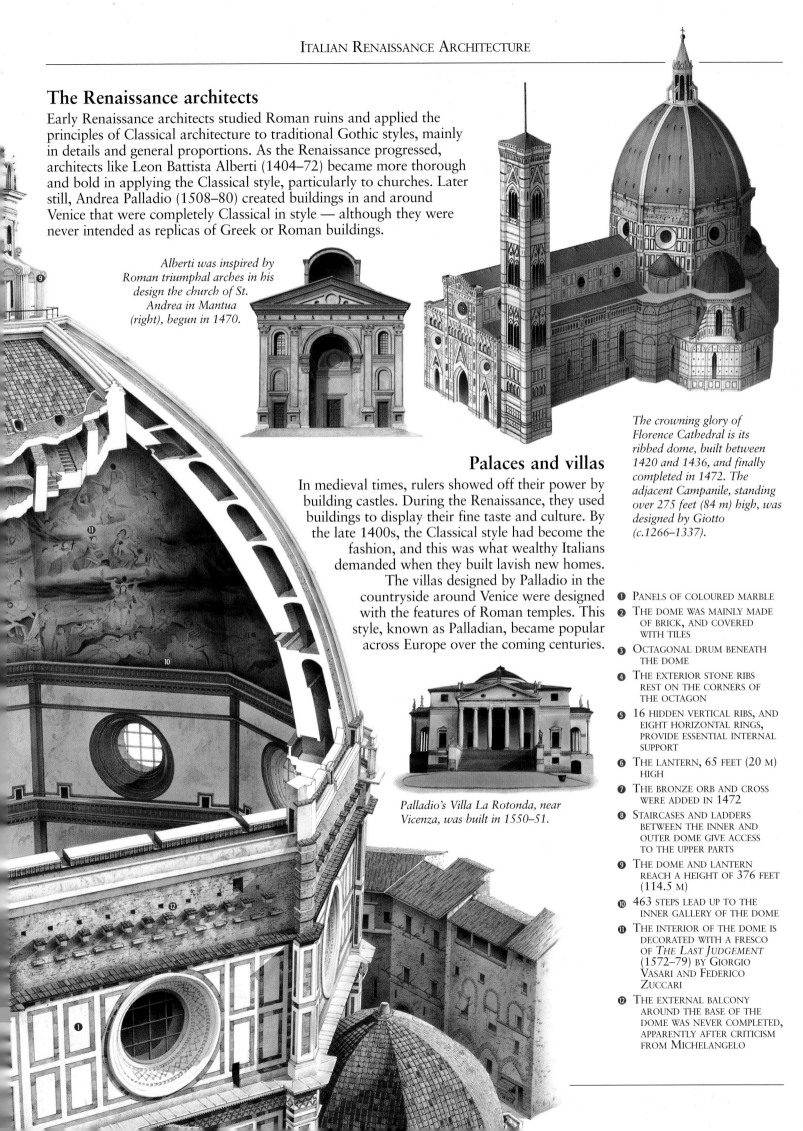

The Renaissance architects

Early Renaissance architects studied Roman ruins and applied the principles of Classical architecture to traditional Gothic styles, mainly in details and general proportions. As the Renaissance progressed, architects like Leon Battista Alberti (1404–72) became more thorough and bold in applying the Classical style, particularly to churches. Later still, Andrea Palladio (1508–80) created buildings in and around Venice that were completely Classical in style — although they were never intended as replicas of Greek or Roman buildings.

Alberti was inspired by Roman triumphal arches in his design the church of St. Andrea in Mantua (right), begun in 1470.

Palaces and villas

In medieval times, rulers showed off their power by building castles. During the Renaissance, they used buildings to display their fine taste and culture. By the late 1400s, the Classical style had become the fashion, and this was what wealthy Italians demanded when they built lavish new homes. The villas designed by Palladio in the countryside around Venice were designed with the features of Roman temples. This style, known as Palladian, became popular across Europe over the coming centuries.

Palladio's Villa La Rotonda, near Vicenza, was built in 1550–51.

The crowning glory of Florence Cathedral is its ribbed dome, built between 1420 and 1436, and finally completed in 1472. The adjacent Campanile, standing over 275 feet (84 m) high, was designed by Giotto (c.1266–1337).

❶ PANELS OF COLOURED MARBLE

❷ THE DOME WAS MAINLY MADE OF BRICK, AND COVERED WITH TILES

❸ OCTAGONAL DRUM BENEATH THE DOME

❹ THE EXTERIOR STONE RIBS REST ON THE CORNERS OF THE OCTAGON

❺ 16 HIDDEN VERTICAL RIBS, AND EIGHT HORIZONTAL RINGS, PROVIDE ESSENTIAL INTERNAL SUPPORT

❻ THE LANTERN, 65 FEET (20 M) HIGH

❼ THE BRONZE ORB AND CROSS WERE ADDED IN 1472

❽ STAIRCASES AND LADDERS BETWEEN THE INNER AND OUTER DOME GIVE ACCESS TO THE UPPER PARTS

❾ THE DOME AND LANTERN REACH A HEIGHT OF 376 FEET (114.5 M)

❿ 463 STEPS LEAD UP TO THE INNER GALLERY OF THE DOME

⓫ THE INTERIOR OF THE DOME IS DECORATED WITH A FRESCO OF *THE LAST JUDGEMENT* (1572–79) BY GIORGIO VASARI AND FEDERICO ZUCCARI

⓬ THE EXTERNAL BALCONY AROUND THE BASE OF THE DOME WAS NEVER COMPLETED, APPARENTLY AFTER CRITICISM FROM MICHELANGELO

The Renaissance City

During the Renaissance, many new and impressive buildings, such as town halls, churches and private palaces were built. Changes were also made to the city landscape, with the clearing away of narrow, crooked and crowded medieval lanes to create squares and wider, straighter streets. There was much discussion about what was the ideal city — a spacious city designed anew from the ground up.

Above: A painting from about 1480 shows an imaginary ideal Renaissance city, empty of people.

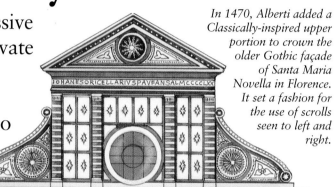

In 1470, Alberti added a Classically-inspired upper portion to crown the older Gothic façade of Santa Maria Novella in Florence. It set a fashion for the use of scrolls seen to left and right.

Italian cities

Civic pride drove the cities of Italy to compete to be not only the most attractive, but also the most civilized. Florence, Urbino, Ferrara, Mantua and Rome all underwent substantial renovation during the Renaissance period. In Ferrara, Duke Ercole I (reigned 1471–1505) almost doubled the size of the city with a new quarter designed by Biagio Rossetti (c.1447–1516), with the result that Ferrara has been called 'the first modern city of Europe'. Rome was reborn in the 1500s, with work at the Vatican focusing on the huge new St. Peter's Basilica.

In Urbino, Federico da Montefeltro set about creating an ideal palace, following the designs of the architect Francesco Laurana (c. 1430–1502).

Right: A medallion showing the portrait of Leon Battista Alberti, from about 1450.

Cities of northern Europe

No cities of northern Europe were completely transformed by the Renaissance, but many — such as Augsburg, Nuremberg, Prague and Paris — show Renaissance influence in individual buildings, squares and broad streets. Italian architects and sculptors were invited to work in northern Europe, notably by the French king Francis I, who was passionate about the Italian Renaissance.

This French architectural decoration, sculpted in terracotta, shows the clear influence of Renaissance Florence.

Planning the ideal city

One of the first architects to pay attention to urban planning was Leon Battista Alberti, who addressed the subject in his influential book *De re aedificatoria* (*About Building Matters*). Published in 1485, it was the first printed book on architecture. Many architects and artists thought about creating the ideal city, including Leonardo da Vinci who, in about 1488, made drawings for a city on a series of levels, each with its own function.

Pienza

In 1459, Pope Pius II (pope 1458–64) decided to transform his birthplace, a hilltop village called Pienza in Tuscany, into an ideal city. His architect was Bernardo Rossellino (1409–64), who had worked with Alberti. The central square of Pienza is surrounded by the town's most important buildings, including the Palazzo Piccolomini (his family residence). Even though Pius' plan for Pienza was never completely carried out, what remains is a significant testimony of the enlightened Renaissance patron's attempts to build the perfect city.

Left: A 1589 print of Pope Sixtus V (pope 1585–90) illustrates some of the building and engineering projects initiated and planned in Rome during his pontificate.

Pius II was celebrated as a humanist pope; he travelled widely and was also a poet and scholar.

All the major Renaissance cities of northern Italy underwent significant rebuilding.

Pienza Cathedral has the earliest fully Renaissance façade in Tuscany. To the right is the Palazzo Piccolomini.

Religion

During medieval times and the early Renaissance, almost all of Europe was Roman Catholic. The Church, with its cathedrals, churches and monasteries, provided the main source of education. It was also wealthy, powerful and very influential. During the Renaissance, however, many people began to feel that the Church was corrupt and hypocritical and had strayed away from the original message of Christianity. A movement developed called Protestantism, which by 1540 had split the Church.

The jewel-studded crown of Pope Julius II (pope 1503–13) is an indication of the great wealth of the Church.

Martin Luther (above) preached that the true guides to religious questions were God, faith and the Bible, not the pope.

The Reformation

In 1517, a German monk and priest called Martin Luther (1483–1546) published his *Ninety-five Theses*, a criticism of Church practices. Luther was simply trying to reform the Church from within, but the Church reacted harshly. Many other critics of the Church sympathized with Luther's complaints, such as the Swiss priest Ulrich Zwingli (1484–1531) and the French lawyer John Calvin (1509–64). Their followers broke away from the Roman Catholic Church in what became known as the Protestant Reformation.

One of the Church abuses singled out by Luther was the sale of 'indulgences' — documents that declared that their purchasers did not have to do penance for their sins.

Counter-Reformation

The Reformation caused great damage to the Catholic Church, weakening its authority and self-esteem. The Church began to address the criticisms in a series of meetings called the Council of Trent (1545–63), which succeeded in making the Church more unified and developing measures of self-reform. This effort to fight the rising tide of Protestantism was called the Counter-Reformation.

Pope Paul III (pope 1534–49) summoned delegates to Trento in Italy in 1545 for the first meetings of the Council of Trent.

Rome and the papacy

Between 1378 and 1417 the Roman Catholic Church had two rival popes, one in Rome and one in Avignon, in southern France. This split is known as the Great Schism. When the dispute was resolved, the papacy returned to Rome, restoring power and prestige to the Church. Before long, popes were introducing Renaissance culture to the Eternal City.

Pope Sixtus IV (pope 1471–84) was a patron of Renaissance art.

Monastic life

There were several long-established monastic orders during the Renaissance. The Benedictines, Carthusians and Cistercians lived isolated in monasteries and devoted themselves to prayer and contemplation. Meanwhile, the Dominicans and Franciscans lived among the community, serving as preachers and social workers. Nuns were similarly divided according to their orders. Although most monks and nuns were pious and dedicated, there were plenty who were greedy, lazy, corrupt and ill-educated.

Above: The Dominican monastery of San Marco in Florence, as depicted in a 15th-century manuscript, shows the monks' spacious courtyards and gardens.

Monks and nuns played a number of key roles in society, such as teaching, distributing welfare to the poor and running hospitals and hostels for pilgrims.

Religious festivals

Many religious festivals were held throughout the year and were often marked by elaborate processions involving the entire community. They included local saint's days and annual celebrations commemorating miracles or giving thanks for military victory. Some were joyous feasts; others were sombre and serious occasions.

A detail from a painting by Gentile Bellini (1429–1507) shows a relic from Christ's cross being paraded through St. Mark's Square in Venice on the feast of Corpus Christi.

Religious images

Throughout medieval times, art was almost entirely religious. During the Renaissance, the rediscovered Classical art was given a Christian meaning, allowing artists to spread and strengthen the message of Christianity through their work. Some Protestant groups, however, opposed religious imagery of any kind.

Above: The Virgin and Child by the Florentine painter Masaccio (1401–28) depicts a theme that remained central to the Roman Catholic Church.

Education

Education received greater attention during the Renaissance and new universities sprang up all over Europe. Gradually both Church schools and universities were available not only to those going into the Church, but also to those planning careers in government administration, medicine, the law and teaching. However, education during the Renaissance was still only accessible to a small and privileged part of society.

Right: The Laurentian Library in Florence was one of the finest libraries of the Renaissance. Originally founded by Cosimo de' Medici the Elder (1389–1464), its new home was designed by Michelangelo in 1524, but not completed until 1571.

Pope Sixtus IV created a new building for the Vatican Library in 1475. In the reading rooms, the books were laid on desks.

Libraries

In medieval times, virtually all libraries belonged to the Church. As the Renaissance progressed, princes, dukes, bishops and wealthy individuals began to collect books, which they often left to universities. Donations of books by Humfrey, Duke of Gloucester formed the basis of the Bodleian Library at Oxford University. The Vatican Library, founded in 1450 by Pope Nicolas V, became one of the greatest libraries in the world.

● *university founded 1401–1500*

● *university founded 1501–1700*

Many new universities were founded across Europe during the Renaissance period.

Right: Louise Labé (1524–66) was a French poetess, who published a book of love sonnets in 1555.

Women scholars

Educated women were highly influential, but rare in the Renaissance period. The Venetian-born poet and writer Christine de Pisan (1364–1431) received a good education at the court of King Charles V of France, where her father served as astrologer. Queen Isabella of Spain (1451–1504) actively encouraged humanist scholarship, while Isabella d'Este (1474–1539) was one of the most scholarly women of her time.

Schools

Few children went to school in Renaissance times. The children of wealthy merchants and the ruling classes had tutors and some gifted boys attended small grammar schools. Others received an education as apprentices in trade guilds. Girls were generally not educated at all. The situation, however, was beginning to change. Humanists, such as the Spanish scholar Juan Luis Vivès (1492-1540) advocated setting up schools for the poor, and the first such schools opened in the Netherlands in 1513.

As this German painting from the early 1500s indicates, schools tended to be small, with a handful of pupils to each teacher, sharing a few books.

Left: A plaque from the 1430s shows a teacher giving a grammar lesson to two boys.

New subjects

The traditional subjects taught at university were theology and philosophy and the seven 'liberal arts': grammar, arithmetic, logic, music, astronomy, geometry and rhetoric. The background theme to all of these was Christianity. However, new subjects gradually entered the curriculum, such as law, medicine, Classical literature, geography and map-making, and the kind of advanced mathematics promoted by Luca Pacioli (c.1445–c.1517), a leading mathematician of the day. But changes were slow in coming.

Many science books, such as this manual on astronomy (above), were based on the work that Greek scholars had done over 1,000 years before.

Universities

The first important European universities — such as those of Oxford, Cambridge, Bologna and Paris — were founded in medieval times. They expanded during the Renaissance and provided the models for the new universities. By 1500 more than 70 had been founded. Demand for places increased as it became the practice for wealthy families to send their sons to university. Some universities even took students from the age of 12. Most teaching took the form of lectures or readings.

Above: Sir Thomas More was England's best-known humanist as well as a leading statesman.

Benozzo Gozzoli's (1420–97) fresco St. Augustine Teaching in Rome depicts him in the guise of a Renaissance university lecturer.

Humanist scholars

The first humanists were Italian, but during the 1500s northern European scholars began to come into their own. The most celebrated was the Dutch priest Desiderius Erasmus (1469–1536). He travelled widely — Paris, Brussels, Turin, London, Oxford, Cambridge and Basel — and made friends with many other humanists. One of these was Thomas More (1477–1535), who wrote *Utopia*, describing an imaginary ideal state founded on reason.

Above: Erasmus did much to free intellectual thought from the restricted view of traditional Christian teaching and superstition.

Renaissance Art

The Renaissance period saw dramatic changes in both painting and sculpture, and produced some of the greatest artists of all time, such as Jan van Eyck, Leonardo da Vinci, Michelangelo, Raphael and Hans Holbein. The rediscovery of the technical brilliance and life-like qualities of Classical sculpture were a challenge to Renaissance sculptors. At the same time, Renaissance painters tried to intensify the realistic qualities of their work.

Above: The German artist Albrecht Dürer (1471–1528) is depicted using a grid to make an accurate perspective drawing of a model.

Sculpture

Early Renaissance artists could see that ancient Greek and Roman sculpture was far more sophisticated than anything produced since then. The first sculptor to challenge this heritage was Donatello, a friend of Alberti, Brunelleschi and Masaccio. He, and later Michelangelo (1475–1564), revived the skills of life-like and anatomically accurate sculpture.

Left: Michelangelo's David *made a powerful statement about the natural dignity and beauty of the human form.*

In The Funeral of St. Stephen, *part of a fresco cycle by Fra Filippo Lippi (c.1406–69), all the architectural lines point towards the vanishing point.*

Perspective

A painting has a flat, two-dimensional surface, but since ancient times artists have known that it is possible to create the illusion of three-dimensional space by using 'perspective'. During the 1400s architects and artists discovered the mathematical rules behind perspective painting, based on the 'vanishing point', to which all horizontal lines are directed.

Michelangelo worked virtually alone on the Sistine Chapel ceiling. It took him four years to complete, much of which was spent standing on a scaffold 66 feet (20 m) above the ground.

Frescoes

Italians used the ancient technique of applying watercolour paint onto fresh (fresco) plaster before it dried. It was a tricky and awkward technique; nonetheless, many frescoes adorned the walls of Renaissance churches and palaces.

Left: A detail from a group of elaborate frescoes in the Palazzo Schifanoia, in Ferrara, depicts the Roman deities Mars and Venus.

Right: Jan van Eyck's wedding portrait (1434) for Giovanni Arnolfini, an Italian merchant in Bruges.

Oil painting

In the early 1400s, northern European artists such as Jan van Eyck (c.1390–1441) perfected the use of oil paint. This could be applied to wooden panels or canvas to make small, portable — and easily sellable — paintings. Oil painting also allowed the kind of detail, shading and rich colouring found in manuscript illustrations. It soon became popular in Italy, and was adopted by artists such as Leonardo da Vinci (1452–1519) and Giovanni Bellini (c.1430–1516).

Portraits

The Renaissance also saw a growing interest in recording the appearance of living people. Artists like Leonardo da Vinci sought to make their sitters look life-like by using delicate shading based on close observation. Renaissance portraits are notable for their naturalism, which sometimes ends up being very unflattering.

Leonardo da Vinci's portrait of Cecilia Gallerani (c.1485) shows her in a relaxed and natural pose.

The Sistine Chapel

Like many Renaissance artists, Michelangelo was multi-talented. In 1508 Pope Julius II commissioned him to paint the entire ceiling of the Sistine Chapel in the Vatican, in Rome. The result was one of the greatest triumphs of Renaissance art — 40 panels of scenes from the Old Testament of the Bible.

❶ THE UNDER-DRAWING WAS SKETCHED IN CHARCOAL AND RED CHALK ONTO THE BASE LAYER OF ROUGH PLASTER

❷ AT THE BEGINNING OF EACH DAY, FRESH PLASTER WAS WAS PLACED OVER A SEGMENT OF THE UNDER-DRAWING

❸ PAINT WAS APPLIED DIRECTLY ONTO THE DAMP PLASTER

❹ THE SHADING AND TONES OF FACES AND CLOTHING WERE CREATED IN THREE LAYERS OF PAINT

❺ THE PAINT WAS MADE OF GROUND PIGMENT MIXED WITH WATER

❻ BLENDING THE PAINT WAS DIFFICULT: SHADING WAS OFTEN ACHIEVED BY STROKES OF DARKER COLOUR

❼ THE TOTAL SIZE OF THE CEILING IS 5,759 SQUARE FEET (535 SQ M)

❽ MICHELANGELO PAINTED VERY MUSCULAR FIGURES

❾ SCAFFOLDING

❿ ASSISTANTS

⓫ THE CEILING WAS INAUGURATED ON 1 NOVEMBER 1512

Michelangelo was renowned for his fiery temper and unkempt appearance.

Artists and Artisans

During the Renaissance, an artist was expected not only to be able to paint or sculpt, but also to have the skills of a goldsmith, and to be able to design buildings, military equipment, theatre sets and stained glass. Brunelleschi, for example, trained as a goldsmith and sculptor, although he was most famous as an architect. Being an artist required training from an early age in a workshop. Fully trained artists belonged to a guild, which among other things, ensured that workshops were properly run.

Vasari's second edition of The Lives of the Artists, *published in 1568.*

Many Renaissance artists began training as goldsmiths. A stained-glass window (c.1480) in Milan Cathedral shows St. Eligius, the 7th-century patron saint of metalworkers, who was apprenticed to a goldsmith in Limoges, France.

Renaissance artists

The first book on the history of the great artists of the Italian Renaissance was written by Giorgio Vasari (1511–74), himself a painter and architect. Called *The Lives of the Artists* (first edition 1550), much of it was based on first-hand reports. He traced the progression of art from the Florentine painter Giotto through to the great names of Italian art, such as the sculptor Lorenzo Ghiberti (1378–1445) and the painters Masaccio (1401–28), Mantegna and Sandro Botticelli (1445–1510). It ended with the High Renaissance artists such as Leonardo, Michelangelo, Raphael (1483–1520) and Titian (c.1490–1576).

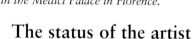

As an indication of his status, the artist Benozzo Gozzoli depicted himself (with his name on his cap) alongside the Medici in a fresco in the Medici Palace in Florence.

Self-portraits

Self-portraiture reflects a humanistic approach to art. Ghiberti included a portrait of himself among his famous bronze relief sculptures on the doors of the Florence Baptistery. Artists would sometimes include portraits of themselves alongside their patrons in religious or mythological scenes.

Raphael painted a self-portrait (right) in 1506, aged 23, when working in Florence.

The status of the artist

In the early Renaissance, artists worked as part of a team. Paintings were made by several contributors working in collaboration and were not signed. Later, the best artists became individually recognized, and they began to sign their paintings. They were treated with respect and honour by their patrons.

Apprentices and assistants

Boys as young as seven could begin training as artists in workshops. At the age of about 13, apprentices began to assist in projects undertaken by the workshop, perhaps doing the backgrounds of paintings, while the master painted the main figures. Around the age of 18, their training was complete. Some continued to work in the master's workshop; the more gifted might become independent artists, with a studio of their own.

Right: This wooden chest, from a Florentine workshop of the 1400s, has been decorated with the care and attention to detail normally reserved for a full-sized painting.

The workshop

Successful artists ran large workshops making a variety of handcrafted products, including pottery tiles and relief sculptures, items in gold and silver, painted book covers, clocks and candlesticks. This huge range of tasks meant that apprentices had to learn an equally broad range of skills — not just drawing, painting, carving, metalwork, how to mix paints and sharpen chisels, but also mathematics, the theory of perspective and basic engineering. Much of the work was commissioned by patrons, but workshops also produced paintings, sculpture and other items for general sale.

Some workshops specialized in casting statues, such as this gilt-bronze Madonna and Child (left), made in the 1400s at a workshop in Salzburg, Austria.

Lorenzo de' Medici (1449–92) was patron to a number of artists, including the young Michelangelo.

Patronage

An essential aspect of Renaissance art was the role of the patrons, who spent huge amounts of money on art — their own money, or sometimes that of their city or the Church. Not only did they provide income and security for artists, but they also had a direct influence on taste in art. The career of Leonardo da Vinci owed much to his patron for 18 years, Duke Ludovico Sforza of Milan (duke 1494–1500).

Under the watchful eye of a skilled master, young apprentices learned a variety of tasks, such as drawing from a live model, grinding colours for paint and preparing wooden panels for painting.

Sculptors had few other tools beside their chisels and their own sheer physical energy.

France, Spain and Portugal

Renaissance ideas and fashions were freely exchanged by means of trade, travelling scholars, diplomatic missions and warfare. By the late 1400s, the Renaissance had taken root in France, Spain and Portugal. Humanist scholars promoted Classical learning at the universities, while the royal courts and nobility adapted Renaissance styles for their lavish palaces and became important patrons of the arts.

Renaissance France

After the end of the Hundred Years' War in 1453, France re-emerged with new confidence. A passion for the Italian Renaissance was led by the young and energetic King Francis I (reigned 1515–47). France's most original contributions, however, were in the field of literature, with profound and amusing philosophical works and poetry — often inspired by Classical works — by authors such as François Rabelais (c.1483–1553) and Michel de Montaigne (1533–92).

The Classical scholar Guillaume Budé (1467–1540) was among the many teachers who helped to make Paris a centre of humanist learning.

Below: El Greco's painting of St Martin and the Beggar shows the elongated figures typical of Mannerism.

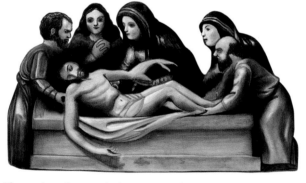

Above: A sculpture of Christ's entombment from the 1500s reflects the strong religious undercurrent of Spain.

A manuscript illustration dated 1484 shows Ferdinand and Isabella as equal partners in their rule over Spain.

The Spanish Renaissance

When Ferdinand of Aragon and Isabella of Castile married in 1469, the stage was set for the unification of Spain and a golden age of stability and culture. Through royal marriage, Spain later acquired a vast empire in Europe. Protestantism in Germany and the Netherlands, however, became an increasing source of conflict, especially under Philip II (reigned 1556–98), and the ideals of Renaissance humanism became increasingly entangled in Catholicism. Mannerist painters like El Greco (1541–1614) helped to reinforce the strong Catholic passions of Spain.

Independent Portugal

Since 1249 Portugal had been an independent country. During the 1400s, humanists arrived from Spain and Italy, leading to a cultural 'golden age' during the reign of Manuel I (reigned 1495–1521). The ornate local style of Gothic architecture, perhaps influenced by the Arabs, gradually merged with Renaissance styles.

By 1530, Lisbon had worldwide links, thanks to the recent exploration by Portuguese navigators.

Work began on transforming the château of Fontainebleau in the late 1520s. A bird's eye view of Fontainebleau shows the Oval Court, where the apartments of Francis I were located.

The French court

Francis I styled himself as a Renaissance prince. He collected paintings, sculpture, books and manuscripts. He brought numerous Italian craftsmen and artists to France, including Leonardo da Vinci. They helped on Francis' building projects, which included remodelling the château at Fontainebleau, near Paris, in the Renaissance style. The château housed his extensive collection of Renaissance art, which included paintings by Raphael and sculptures by Michelangelo.

In a miniature of about 1530, Francis I and his court are seen listening to a reading by a scholar, part of his daily routine.

Francis I also built a magnificent Renaissance palace at Chambord (below), in the Loire Valley.

The Renaissance had an impact in many parts of France, Spain and Portugal.

Architecture

During the 1400s, the rulers of France and Spain were still building fortresses. In the more stable 1500s, they wanted palaces. These were designed along the lines of the Renaissance palaces in Italy, with Classical influence in the proportions, the use of arches and details such as pilasters and pediments. Philip II's vast palace near Madrid, the Escorial (built 1563–84), was designed in a severe Classical style, reflecting his austere sense of piety.

Antwerp in Flanders was the most important trading and commercial centre in western Europe in the late 15th century. By the 1550s, it had over 100,000 inhabitants, the majority of whom worked in trade or the city's many industries — including breweries, sugar refineries and silk and tapestry factories.

Above: Many cities of Germany and the Low Countries became prosperous through trade during the Renaissance period.

Northern Renaissance cities

Cities such as Bruges and Ghent in the Low Countries were among the biggest and most prosperous in Europe during the Renaissance period. Although largely self-governing, during the late 1300s they came under the control of the Dukes of Burgundy, who brought peace and stability and established a glittering court in Bruges. In Germany, the cities thrived on trade, as well as the wealth generated by bankers such as the Fugger. As in Italy, the cities of northern Europe became the centres of a flourishing cultural life.

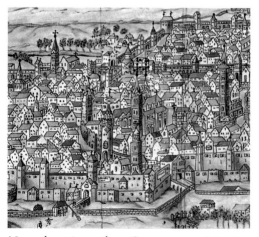

Nuremberg, in southern Germany, was Dürer's birthplace and where he spent much of his life.

Textile industry

In northern Europe, textiles was the most important industry involving international trade. Some of the best wool came from England and was exported to the Low Countries, where it was made into fine cloth. The wealthy cities in the Low Countries, such as Bruges and Brussels, specialized in luxury cloth, and workshops produced costly tapestries that decorated the walls of palaces throughout Europe. The defence of the cloth trade was even the cause of political treaties, royal marriages and international conflict in the early Renaissance.

Brussels was famous for its tapestries. Many were designed by the best artists of the day.

Craftsmanship

The wealth of the merchants and bankers of northern Europe provided a ready market for fine goods, such as textiles, furniture, silverware, tapestry, jewellery and paintings. Goldsmiths and silversmiths were skilled craftsmen, who often turned their hand to other forms of technical innovation; Gutenberg, for instance, trained as a goldsmith. Paintings of the 1400s by Bruges-based artists such Jan van Eyck and Hans Memling (c.1430–94) reveal a world glittering with all kinds of precious material goods.

A German drinking vessel, made of an exotic seashell, in a silver gilt stand.

Dürer and Bruegel

Painting traditions had been strong in northern Europe since medieval times. This continued into the 1500s, when the influence of the Italian Renaissance and humanism reached a peak. Among the greatest talents were the German Albrecht Dürer (1471–1528) and the Flemish painter Pieter Bruegel the Elder (1525–69). Both made journeys to Italy to study painting.

Dürer revealed the potential of printmaking as an art form; his technical mastery can be seen in this woodcut (above) entitled St. Christopher *(1511).*

Left: Peasants dancing at a wedding in a detail of a painting by Bruegel. It shows Bruegel's interest in the ordinary people of Flanders.

Germany and the Low Countries

In Germany and the Low Countries, the Renaissance was essentially an intellectual movement, fuelled by humanist scholars such as Erasmus, the new universities and the printing revolution. By the early 1500s, the so-called 'Northern Renaissance' had begun to rival that of Italy. These countries, made wealthy through trade, had a strong middle class of rich merchants. Oil painting flourished in the 1400s, but architecture did not show the influence of the Renaissance until the late 1500s. By this time, religious strife had begun to tear northern Europe apart.

The Holy Roman Empire

In 1519 Charles V (1500–58) found himself ruler of a vast European empire, consisting of the Netherlands, parts of Germany, Italy and Spain. He was from the Austrian Habsburg family, which had inherited the old title of Holy Roman Emperor, and saw himself as the defender of Catholic values. The end of his reign, however, coincided with the growing conflict with Protestants.

Left: Emperor Maximilian I, here in a painting by Dürer, gained the Low Countries for the Habsburg family by marriage in 1477. He was the grandfather of Charles V.

The Merchant's House

In cities across Europe, wealthy merchants built grand town houses, where work and family life often intermingled. Merchants conducted business from their homes, and tradesmen often lived above their workshops. Success brought the comfort of fine living, and the time and money for education and the pursuit of Renaissance culture in books, art and music.

Merchants

The merchants of the Renaissance made money by buying goods and selling them at a profit. Wealthy merchants could also speculate by funding overseas trading ventures in return for a share of the profits, or by trading in these shares at the new stock exchanges. As more and more trading ships began to sail to Asia and the Americas, the potential for huge profits grew, along with the risk of disaster through shipwreck or other misfortunes.

Left: An English merchant of around 1590. Merchants were among the wealthiest and most powerful people in Europe.

❶ HOUSE FRAME WAS MADE OF WOODEN TIMBERS, FILLED IN WITH BRICK, PLASTER AND STRAW

❷ GROUND FLOOR OF WORKSHOPS, OFFICES, WAREHOUSES AND SHOPS

❸ WINDOWS

❹ VALUABLE POSSESSIONS WERE KEPT IN LOCKED CHESTS

❺ OIL LAMPS AND CANDLES

❻ BEDROOM

❼ CURTAINS WERE HUNG AROUND THE BED FOR WARMTH, DARKNESS AND PRIVACY

❽ KITCHEN

❾ FIREPLACE

❿ STOOLS AND BENCHES

⓫ SERVANTS AND CHILDREN OFTEN SLEPT AT THE TOP OF THE HOUSE

⓬ ROOF

A French street shows the houses of prosperous merchants standing one next to the other near the centre — close to the markets where goods were traded.

Renovation and renewal

A successful merchant could afford to improve his home. During the Renaissance, many medieval city houses were refurbished, embellished with classical details and larger windows added. Some merchants completely rebuilt their houses. In Florence, this meant building in the stone styles pioneered by Brunelleschi and Alberti; in the Low Countries, new houses were built of brick, with step-gables at the roof-line, and façades decorated with Renaissance motifs. The very wealthy also built country mansions; in France, châteaux were built in styles that reflected the Italian influences introduced by Francis I.

Right: The Palazzo Davanzati, dating to the 1300s, is a fine example of the kind of merchant's house built in Florence. The top floor loggia, which provided a sheltered space for sitting out in summer, was added in the Renaissance.

Above: This Italian textile shop of the late 1400s, may well have occupied the ground floor of a merchant's house.

Inside the house

The ground floor was often devoted to business. The family lived upstairs, where the main reception rooms were found. In northern countries, the walls of grander houses were decorated with tapestries, which also kept in the warmth. Merchants also tended to use cheaper wooden panelling, or embossed Spanish leather, which was hung like wallpaper.

Furniture remained basically plain and functional, but was often embellished with carved relief, as seen in this chair of the 1500s.

Music was an essential part of any Renaissance gathering. Here the musicians are playing the lute and pan-pipes.

Fashion

The wealthy and powerful used clothing as a way of showing off their status. Complex weaving, dyeing and embroidery techniques were developed to fashion elaborate textiles made of the highest-quality wools and silk. The result was often spectacular and worn with equal pride by men and women. With the rise of Protestantism and the Counter-Reformation, however, such extravagance began to be frowned upon. This sentiment was expressed in the growing fashion for wearing black, in which Charles V and Philip II led by example.

A detail from an Italian fresco of the mid-1400s depicts a man dressed in fashionable clothes of the time.

Music

Music was an important part of the Renaissance world, and an area in which women were permitted to excel. Musical instruments of the period included the lute, harpsichord, portable organ, viola, cello, various wind instruments and drums. Singing also played a key role in music-making. Successful musicians and composers performed at courts around Europe. The Flemish composer Josquin des Prés (c.1450–1521), for instance, worked in Milan, Rome, Paris and Ferrara. More and more secular music — such as love ballads — was also being produced, which was circulated by means of printed music.

Right: A small group gather to play music in this detail from a 16th century painting.

Renaissance Culture

For most people in the Renaissance, life was hard, unpredictable and often short. Any opportunity to have fun was greatly welcomed. With this in mind, the rulers staged spectacular public events to mark special occasions. When Charles the Bold, Duke of Burgundy, married Margaret of York in 1468, festivities included costumed parades, fountains flowing with wine and a whale that opened up to reveal a troupe of 40 performers.

Dutch artist Jan Mostaert (c.1475- c.1555) depicts a game in which the contestant had to dance round a raw egg without breaking it.

Left: A bronze candlestick in the form of a court jester. These clown-like characters were paid to entertain the court.

Sports and pastimes

Among the nobility, most forms of exercise involved some kind of hunting or weapons-practice, such as fencing, archery and jousting. Popular sports such as football and horse-racing were usually informal events, played to local rules. The wealthy also developed an interest in creating pleasure gardens.

Above: In Florence, contestants face up to each other for the physical game called civettino (little owl).

Entertainment

At a time when only a few could read, people devised their own forms of entertainment. They danced, sang, told stories and recited poetry, played board-games and dice. Entertainment at court was more lavish. Poetry-readings and music recitals might be mixed with performances by clowns, acrobats, contortionists and jugglers. Animals were also used in cock-fighting and bear-baiting.

Festivals

Saints' days and other celebrations were marked by lavish festivals, often staged in the public squares of the cities. Events might include processions, jousting tournaments, horseraces, mock battles, theatrical performances and fireworks displays. As Bruegel suggests in his paintings, festivities were not limited to the city: villagers also enjoyed dances, music, eating and drinking. In the Low Countries, each village celebrated the feast day of its patron saint with a 'kermis' — a combination of a fair and a festival.

Falconry — the ancient practice of hunting for game with trained birds of prey — was a popular pastime of the wealthy.

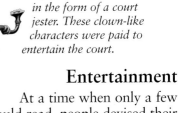

A variety of performers entertain the crowd at a festival in the Piazza Santo Spirito, in Florence.

Food and drink

People ate the food that was in season. Only the wealthy could indulge in extravagant dishes. Most of today's foods were available, although tomatoes, potatoes, peppers and most kinds of beans and chocolate only arrived in the 16th century, brought from America (see pages 44–45). Wine was generally drunk in the south, beer in the north, but trade also brought wine to northern Europe.

Above: Wine drinkers are pictured in a detail from a fresco by Giotto in Padua, Italy.

Clothes and jewellery

During the Renaissance, wealthy women wore elaborate gowns, which were long, sweeping the ground and almost always thick and heavy. These complex garments, often encrusted with jewels, required great skill and considerable labour to wash, starch and iron. The wealthy had servants to do this. Family wealth was often invested in jewellery. A great deal of skilled craftsmanship went into fashioning rings, necklaces, brooches and ornaments for the hair.

Venetian platform shoes of the 1400s allowed the wearer to keep her dress above the dirt and puddles.

Children

Most children were born into large families, with perhaps ten or more brothers and sisters. The older children usually looked after the younger ones, until they were old enough to find paid work or start training for a trade. Most did not go to school. The period between infancy and adulthood was usually very short.

A glazed terracotta head of a boy by the Florentine sculptor Andrea della Robbia.

Right: This ring from central Europe shows the heart — symbol of love — held by two hands.

Above: A gold and enamel brooch from the Netherlands, dating to about 1450, depicts a bridal couple.

Working women

The vast majority of women came from the lower working class and had to work. They were employed as farm labourers, maids, cooks, nurses for infants, washerwomen, market traders, embroiderers and dressmakers. Many also helped their husbands to run their businesses. Women of the middle class and the nobility were fully occupied in running their households, but generally lived in more comfortable circumstances.

A German painting shows women washing clothes in a river.

Education and status

It was only during the late 1500s, under the influence of humanist thinking, that girls began to attend school. Earlier, some women had been educated privately, but they were generally from the nobility and upper classes. Some became writers, poets and musicians, but they were the exception. Renaissance humanists discussed the concept of the equality of the sexes, and the role of women in society was widely debated. In practice, however, women were generally considered inferior to men.

There is some evidence that women of wealthy families were taught to paint; this manuscript illustration (right) of the 1400s shows a woman painting a self-portrait.

Above: Many Renaissance women spent their lives surrounded by babies and children.

Right: The marriage in 1533 of Caterina de' Medici (1519–89) and the future king of France, Henry II (1519–59), was considered a good catch for the Medici family of Florence.

A group of wealthy Renaissance women read and play games with their children.

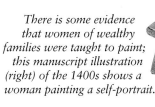

Marriage and family

Marriages were often arranged by the parents, choosing for their son or daughter a partner who might bring them greater status or money. Marriages between ruling families were considered a good way to seal the relationship between two nations. Love was not a prime concern in these arrangements. A woman left her own home to live in the home of her husband, thus moving from the rule of her father to that of her husband. As part of the marriage settlement, the future wife would give her husband a dowry — a valuable gift of money or property.

Women and Children

In the Renaissance, the goal of most girls was to marry and have children. The primary role of women was that of homemaker. Girls could marry as young as 14 or in their late teens. Then they would start to have children, at the rate of about one a year. As many as two out of three babies would die at birth, or in infancy. Childbirth was also dangerous for the mothers, and many died giving birth, or from complications following it. It is not surprising, therefore, that men controlled most aspects of life outside the family. Women who did not marry usually entered a convent.

Science and Medicine

For much of the Renaissance, science was still largely based on the work of the ancient Greeks over 1,000 years before. This knowledge had also been preserved by the Muslim Arabs. The Renaissance rediscovery of Greek learning marked some advance since the medieval period, while basic scientific knowledge spread quickly after the invention of printing. It was not until the late Renaissance, however, that any great improvements were made on ancient knowledge.

Above: An anatomical drawing by an Arab doctor of the 1400s shows a basic understanding of the internal organs.

Andrea della Robbia sculpted this ceramic roundel (left) for the Ospedale degli Innocenti, the first orphanage in Florence.

A Renaissance hospital was usually housed in a large building, with huge wards lined with beds. The basic needs of the patients were mostly met by their families.

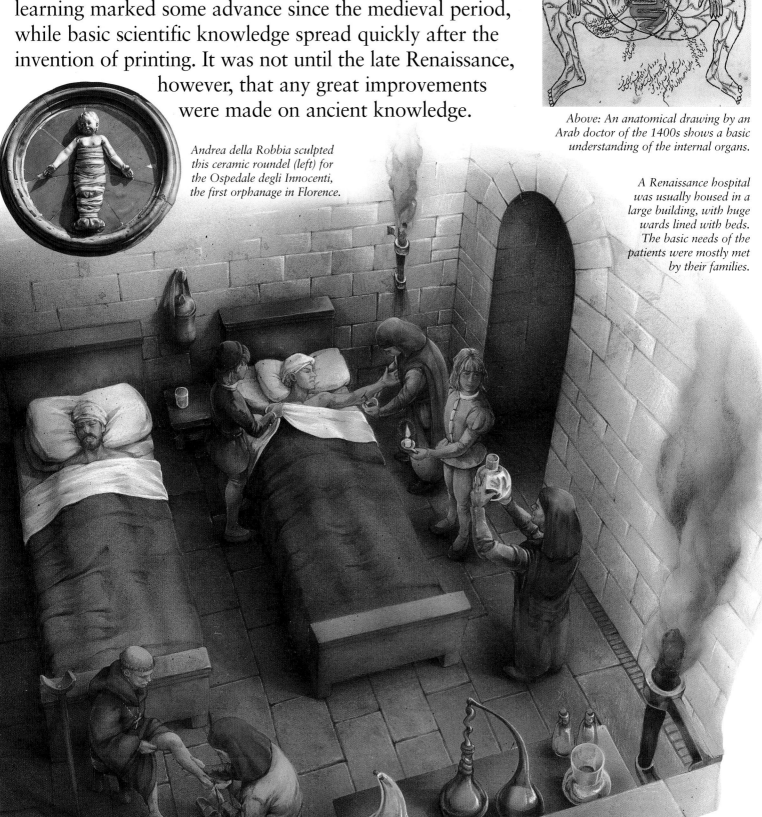

Hospitals

During the Renaissance, virtually all hospitals were run by religious institutions, but often funded by rich patrons or the guilds. As medicines were not powerful enough to bring about a cure, diseases were usually left to take their course, but doctors brought comfort by identifying the disease and predicting its course. Doctors also carried out surgery, but without the aid of anaesthetic. Some hospitals cared for orphans and abandoned children, such as the Ospedale degli Innocenti, founded in Florence in 1419.

The ancient Greek method of bandaging the head is typical of the medical information available in the Renaissance period.

Renaissance pharmacists

Ancient Greek doctors such as Hippocrates (c.460–377 B.C.) had taught the virtues of observing the progress of a patient's illness and the effect of any medicines administered. Since medieval times, monasteries had been following a similar approach. They grew herbs in their gardens and provided a range of medicines. Meanwhile, less reputable pharmacists created many useless potions based on ingredients such as worm's liver or tongue of newt.

Pharmacies like this one (left), from the 1400s, displayed their wares in pots on shelves behind the counter. Renaissance pharmacies were often attached to hospitals.

The alchemist

Gold was the most valuable of all metals. Some people thought that gold contained the secret of eternal life and could provide a universal remedy for all ills, including sin. Some goldsmiths thought it possible to transform ordinary or 'base' metals into gold. This pursuit was called 'alchemy'. Alchemy laid the foundations for the science of chemistry.

Alchemists employed the full range of equipment used by goldsmiths and pharmacists in the forlorn hope of creating gold.

Medicine

Since doctors had only rudimentary knowledge of anatomy, disease and medicine, their work was largely a matter of guesswork, often mixed with superstition. There were, however, plenty of practitioners, such as midwives, who could provide invaluable service based on practical experience. Knowledge was pooled by the universities, and new faculties of medicine were opened where a scientific approach was taught.

Above: It was known that checking urine samples could help in the diagnosis of disease.

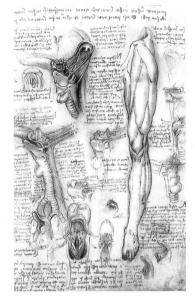

Above: Leonardo da Vinci set a standard for anatomical drawing that was not matched for centuries.

Anatomy

During the early Renaissance period, knowledge of the internal workings of the human body remained incomplete. Advances came with the anatomical research of the Flemish doctor Andreas Vesalius (1514–64). He dissected bodies for his ground-breaking book *De humani corporis fabrica* (*On the Structure of the Human Body*, 1543). Decades earlier, Leonardo da Vinci had filled manuscripts with detailed anatomical drawings based on dissection.

Astronomy

Arab astronomers based their knowledge on Aristotle's mistaken conviction that the Earth lay at the centre of a globe-like Universe. In about 1512, the Polish astronomer Nicolaus Copernicus (1473–1543) realized that this theory was contradicted by his observations. Instead he proposed that the Sun lay at the centre of our planetary system; he published this idea in 1540. It was confirmed by Galileo Galelei (1564–1642), but the Church forced him to deny it.

Above: In 1606 Galileo Galelei became the first astronomer to use a telescope, an instrument recently invented in the Netherlands.

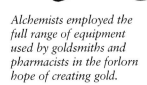

Left: Copernicus' illustration shows the Earth moving around the Sun, an idea that ordinary people, and especially the Church authorities, found hard to accept.

Literature and Theatre

The study of Classical literature and the development of printing, making this material more widely available, inspired many to produce their own literary criticism, philosophical works and poetry. There was also a revival in drama during the period. Plays were performed for royal courts throughout Europe, in the banqueting halls and courtyards of palaces. Temporary stages were also erected in public squares, at fairs and in inns. In the late 1500s plays became so popular with the general public that permanent theatres began to be built.

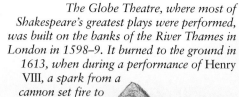

The Globe Theatre, where most of Shakespeare's greatest plays were performed, was built on the banks of the River Thames in London in 1598–9. It burned to the ground in 1613, when during a performance of Henry VIII, *a spark from a cannon set fire to the thatch.*

Rabelais was strongly criticized by the Church, but he was protected by his friend and patron Cardinal du Bellay.

Dramatists, poets and writers

Among the many forms of literature, drama had the advantage of being performed. It therefore appealed to both the uneducated masses and the more cultured audiences. In England, the plays of William Shakespeare (1564–1616), Christopher Marlowe (1564–93) and others were very popular. Elsewhere, writers demonstrated the imaginative creativity of the Renaissance in prose tales of immense scope. François Rabelais (1483–1553) in France wrote the satires *Pantagruel* (1532) and *Gargantua* (1534), and in Spain, Cervantes (1547–1616) produced *Don Quixote* (1605).

❶ ENTRANCE
❷ TIMBER FRAME STRUCTURE
❸ THATCHED ROOF
❹ OPEN-AIR THEATRE
❺ STAGE
❻ ACTORS
❼ THERE WAS LITTLE SCENERY AND NO STAGE CURTAIN
❽ THREE TIERS OF GALLERIES
❾ PLAYS USUALLY TOOK PLACE IN THE AFTERNOON
❿ AUDIENCE
⓫ SOME MEMBERS OF THE AUDIENCE WERE SEATED ON STOOLS ON THE STAGE
⓬ THE CHEAPEST TICKETS PERMITTED 'GROUNDLINGS' TO STAND IN THE OPEN, CLOSE TO THE STAGE
⓭ A FLAG WAS RAISED AT THE START OF A PERFORMANCE

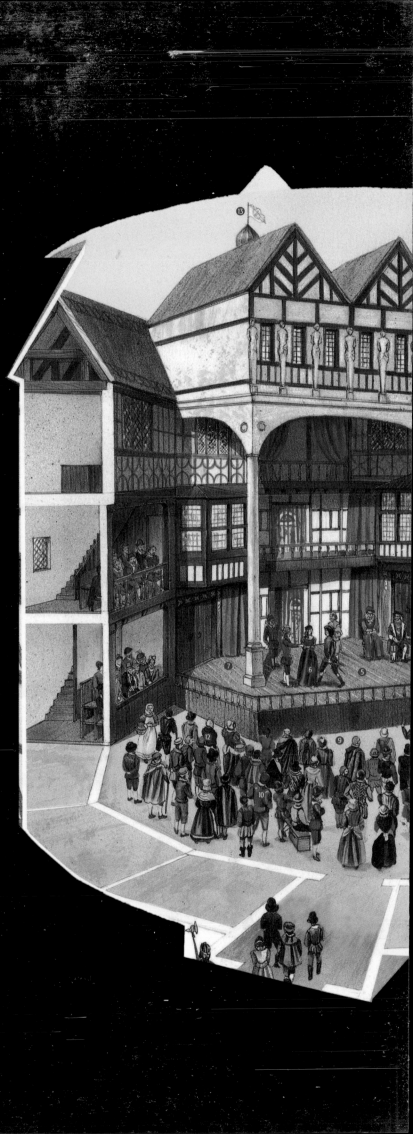

Actors

Until the late Renaissance, acting was not a profitable livelihood. The first professional theatre companies grew out of the Italian *Commedia dell'Arte* tradition in the 1500s. They performed unscripted comedies based around a group of characters, such as Harlequin, Pierrot and Columbine. In England, actors became increasingly professional with the success of the permanent theatres. Only men, however, were permitted to act, so they also had to play the women's roles.

The masked actors in the Commedia dell'Arte *performed a mixture of song, dance, mime and farce.*

Drama and plays

The origins of European theatre lie in ancient Greek drama. This was divided into two forms: comedy and tragedy. Texts of these plays became available during the Renaissance and proved a major inspiration. While audiences liked to be entertained and amused by comedy, they also liked to be drawn into tales of jealousy and blood-soaked murder.

Even after permanent theatres had been built, actors continued to perform on temporary stages on the streets of Elizabethan London.

Below: This drawing of the Swan Theatre, London, made in 1596, is the only existing visual record of the interior of an Elizabethan playhouse.

Theatres

The passion for theatre grew rapidly throughout Europe in the late 1500s. London's first permanent theatre was built in 1576. Architects studied the design of Greek and Roman theatres, adapting these models for interior, roofed spaces. The results became increasingly more ornate and impressive. Palladio's Teatro Olimpico (1586) in Vicenza, Italy was closely designed on a Classical model and is perhaps one of the finest examples of a Renaissance theatre.

Warfare

War was a constant threat in the Renaissance period. While the Italian city-states patronized art and humanist learning, their armies clashed over territory, trade routes and political power. Renaissance genius was also applied to warfare. With the development of gunpowder, weapons became more powerful. When the French king invaded Italy in 1494, his army was equipped with new light and mobile cannons. Rulers throughout Europe began to upgrade their weapons and defences, and the nature of warfare underwent a complete change.

The Florentine artist Paolo Uccello (c.1397–1475) painted Sir John Hawkwood, the respected English condottiere, in the form of an equestrian statue in Florence Cathedral.

Soldiers and armies

In medieval times, the battlefield was dominated by the knight. The improved, armour-piercing power of the crossbow, however, forced a change in tactics, and knights began to be replaced by more mobile cavalry. Professional mercenaries played a major role in the new armies, especially the condottieri in Italy. Armies grew in size: while in 1500 a typical army numbered 30,000, by 1600 it had 60,000 men.

Francis I was captured at the Battle of Pavia in 1525 after his horse was brought down by a firearm. The Habsburg army fielded 1,500 Spanish arquebusiers, and the French army of 28,000 was virtually wiped out.

Military dress

A Renaissance sensitivity to the aesthetically pleasing was also applied to the military, as armour became lighter and more elegant. By 1600, heavy full body armour was only used on ceremonial occasions. Uniforms also became more elaborate. Michelangelo is said to have designed the uniform of the Swiss Guard, the mercenaries who became the bodyguards of the pope.

A helmet of the 1500s shows the craftsmanship of Florentine armourers.

Above: Soldiers carrying firearms march behind pikemen.

Firearms and weapons

Cannons had been used in Europe since the 1200s, but during the early 1500s, hand-held firearms also rose to prominence. The first such firearm was the arquebus, which had a range of 328 feet (100 m); this gave way to the heavier musket, which had to be rested on a fork stick for firing. Cannons, meanwhile, became lighter, more powerful and accurate, and could be dragged into battle on wheels.

Above: Cannons could also be mounted on top of a watchtower, providing 360 degrees of cover.

Defences

With the introduction of more powerful artillery after 1450, medieval fortifications became outdated. The thick stone walls that once protected cities and medieval castles could no longer stand up to an attack. Italian military engineers devised a new kind of fortification to meet this threat: star-shaped earthworks faced with stone, and defended by cannons.

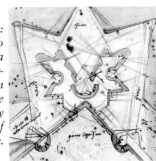

Right: Michelangelo sketched a plan for a star-shaped bastion to protect one of the city gates of Florence.

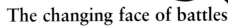

Below: Traditional weapons are shown in this detail of The Battle of San Romano *by Paolo Uccello. Pistols (right) were introduced in the early 1500s.*

War at sea

Cannons also changed the nature of sea-battles. Decks mounted with cannons could devastate enemy ships, even at a distance. The last great sea-battle using oared war-galleys was the Battle of Lepanto of 1571, when the Venetian fleet, with cannons mounted in their bows, defeated the Ottoman Turks off Greece. In 1588, by the time the Spanish Armada sailed the seas, warships had become floating fortresses.

The changing face of battles

France, England and the Habsburg empire of Austria jockeyed for power across Europe for much of the Renaissance period. One of the main battle grounds was Italy, the subject of complex territorial disputes. Clashes between the Habsburgs and France reached a climax at the Battle of Pavia in 1525, when the French army was defeated. This battle was also a turning point in warfare: hand-held firearms began to replace traditional arms, such as swords, bows and lances.

The Spanish Armada was a fleet of 130 ships despatched by Philip II to invade Protestant England.

Voyage and Discovery

In the early Renaissance period, old trade routes bringing spices to Europe were disrupted. As a solution to the problem, the Portuguese, in the 1400s, decided to try and find the source of the spices, which they knew to be in the East, in a land vaguely known as India. However, they had very limited knowledge of the world. The best world map had been produced by Ptolemy in about AD 140 and it did not even show the Americas. By the 1500s, however, knowledge of the world had improved enormously.

Columbus was made Admiral of the Ocean Sea after his triumphant return to Spain in 1493, when he was awarded a coat of arms (above).

Mapmaking and navigation

As explorers made their voyages around the world, their reports were used by mapmakers, to fill in, bit by bit, the empty spaces on the globe. Many early maps were based on speculation and were wildly inaccurate. This was partly because navigators did not have a precise idea of where they were. Their primitive navigational equipment could indicate latitude accurately, but not longitude.

Above: A map of the world of 1590 is given an odd twist by being mounted in a fool's hood.

Right: The Portuguese navigator Vasco da Gama was the first European to find a sea-route to India. He later became a viceroy to Portuguese possessions in India.

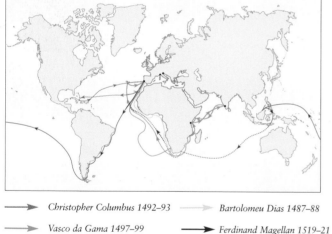

→ Christopher Columbus 1492–93 → Bartolomeu Dias 1487–88

→ Vasco da Gama 1497–99 → Ferdinand Magellan 1519–21

Within a short period of time, European explorers had travelled all around the globe.

Around the world

Within just a few decades, European navigators had reached eastern Asia by sailing eastwards and the Americas by sailing westwards. In 1519 the Spanish navigator Ferdinand Magellan (c.1480–1521) set out with five ships and 270 men to find a westward route to the Spice Islands. It was a gruelling voyage, and Magellan was killed in the Philippines. In 1522 only one ship returned to Portugal, the first to have circumnavigated the world.

Voyages of discovery

Between 1497 and 1499, Vasco da Gama (c.1460–1524) rounded the Cape of Good Hope and reached India. A series of other expeditions followed. Tales of these travels, and the goods that the ships bought back, caused huge excitement. Meanwhile, the Genoese navigator Christopher Columbus (1451–1506), under the sponsorship of Ferdinand and Isabella of Spain, headed westwards in search of India. In 1492 he encountered the Caribbean islands, which became known as the West Indies.

Left: A map of 1545 marks Magellan's voyage around the world. Note the areas of the map that are not yet filled in.

After a 33-day sea crossing in search of the East, Christopher Columbus and his fleet of three ships arrived in San Salvador in October 1492. The native people of the island, the Taìnos, greeted him with surprise and curiosity. The Taìnos people carried no weapons or armour, and often wore earrings, necklaces and bracelets. They were expert weavers, potters and carvers, and cultivated the sweet potato, corn, maize, cotton and pineapples.

Creating empires

Exploration began as a business venture, to find a fast and safe way of getting precious spices. It was also driven by a curiosity to know more about the world. It soon became a ruthless quest for territory, however, as Portugal, Spain, France, England and the Netherlands set out in search of foreign lands to exploit. It resulted in the slave trade and genocidal wars, and it introduced diseases to which native populations had no immunity.

Right: Prince Henry the Navigator (1394–1460) of Portugal made no voyages himself, but he played a vital role in encouraging Portuguese explorers to take a methodical approach to exploration.

Left: Diseases such as measles devastated the native population of the Americas. Between 1500 and 1625 the population of Central America had been reduced from at least 11 million to just 1.25 million.

Seafaring vessels

Trans-ocean exploration became possible through the use of small, sturdy vessels, such as the Portuguese caravel, which had been developed in the 1200s. Just 69 feet (21 m) in length, it could be operated by a crew of 25. In the 1490s, larger and more spacious Mediterranean merchant ships called carracks were used for exploration.

Above: A Portuguese earthenware bowl of 1500 depicts a caravel.

Index